I0902076

Encouraging Words for THOSE WHO *Serve*

warnerpress

3058002100000270

Warner Press, Inc.
Warner Press and Warner Press logo are trademarks of Warner Press, Inc.

Edited by: Julie Campbell
Cover and Layout by: Curtis Corzine

Printed in the USA

One of the greatest rewards that we ever receive for serving God is the permission to do still more for Him.

Charles Spurgeon

I long to

accomplish a

great and noble task,

but it is my chief duty

to accomplish small

tasks as if they were

great and noble.

Helen Keller

Lord, our Lord, how majestic is your name
in all the earth!

Psalm 8:1 (NIV)

One of my responsibilities while working with at-risk children in a church after-school program was to lead the weekly Bible study. In one of our sessions, I looked up the meaning of each child's name. As I called each name individually, I shared the significance and suggested ways he or she might live up to the distinct purpose implied.

In Psalm 8:1, the psalmist declared that God lived up to the name of "Lord." The word "majestic" means greater than anything else. Our Lord rules in majesty with power, glory, and dignity. We cannot look on any of the natural wonders of this world without proclaiming praise and glory to its Creator God. When we observe the beauty of creation, this draws our attention to its Designer. We recognize God as the Architect of all grandeur.

Just as God reflects the glory and beauty of the name "Lord," may we strive to live up to the name "Christian," displaying through our witness and our love for others that we are followers of Christ.

Rev. Rita Hays

God's work

done in God's way

will never lack

God's supply.

Hudson Taylor

This is the day which the LORD hath made; we will rejoice and be glad in it.

PSALM 118:24 (KJV)

Life is a gift best unwrapped slowly, but most days pass by in a blur. Between work, managing a household, appointments, and ministry opportunities, we barely have time to catch a breath.

In times like these we need God's gentle reminder to just slow down. Life isn't about how fast we accomplish our tasks, but about the people we help and the memories we make along the way. Each day is filled with opportunities to make a difference in the world for God. We won't notice them if we are speeding through our days too quickly.

Today, make a conscious effort to slow down and notice God's extraordinary gifts during your ordinary day. You'll be surprised at what a difference it makes!

Small deeds

done are

better than

great deeds

planned.

Rev. Peter Marshall

We have different gifts, according to the grace given to each of us.

Romans 12:6 (niv)

Have you ever gathered shells at the beach? Although you may find two that look alike, upon closer inspection you will find that there is always something different. This is also true about us. Although people may sometimes appear similar in their outward appearance, their talents, or personalities, we too are unique unto ourselves. God's design for our lives also differs for each individual. In Romans 12:6 (niv), Paul teaches us, *We have different gifts, according to the grace given to each of us.* Our Creator made us for a purpose and by serving Him, using the gifts He has given us, we may best use our uniqueness for His glory. Celebrate your God-given talent today, and by doing so, you will reflect your Creator's handiwork.

In this world

it is not what

we take up,

but what we give up,

that makes us rich.

Henry Ward Beecher

You will keep in perfect peace
all who trust in you.

Isaiah 26:3 (NLT)

Clashes in politics, constant changes in the economy, a crumbling moral foundation—no wonder we struggle to stand upright at times, when both our environment and our own emotions crash down on us so often. Yet even in this turbulence, we can trust that our God will never change. Because God remains the same, we can trust Him completely. When we place our confidence in the Lord instead of focusing on the changes around us or even within us, we can find unparalleled peace. Today, instead of focusing on our inadequacies, let's focus on our sufficient God. Thank Him for His unchanging nature and for His promise of perfect peace. Let your thoughts relax as you allow Him to be your steadfast hope in a turbulent world.

Stephanie Hansen

Expect great things from God. Attempt great things for God.

William Carey

Do not fear, for I am with you....
I will strengthen you and help you.

ISAIAH 41:10 (NIV)

When I was a teen, I went on a cave exploration trip with my youth group. Crawling around with flashlights in a cave was exhilarating at first, but some recent rains had transformed the cave floor into a slippery mess. At one point, we had to climb up a steep incline to get to a new level in the cave. As I was almost to the top, my feet started slipping and my hands had nothing to grab but mud. Just when I thought I couldn't hang on any longer, my older brother heard my cries for help, held out his hand, and pulled me up with his strong grasp. The relief I felt was overwhelming!

A similar scenario often plays out in my daily life. Just when I'm at my weakest and ready to give up, Jesus offers me His gentle, helping hand. He looks at me with loving, not scolding, eyes and says, "I'm here, child. I know what you're going through, and I'm going to help you."

Julie Campbell

Do all the good

you can

by all the means you can

in all the places you can

at all the times you can

to all the people you can

as long as ever you can.

John Wesley

Cast all your anxiety on him because
he cares for you.

1 Peter 5:7 (NIV)

The sun streamed through the windowpane at just the right angle to cast the shadow of a cross on the opposite wall. As the sun rose, the cross faded, then disappeared. Even though I start each day focused on Scripture reading and prayer, laying my burdens at the foot of the cross, many times as the day progresses, I pick those cares and burdens up again, and the power of the cross fades away just as quickly as that shadow.

We magnify what we focus on, so when we concentrate on our cares and concerns, the power of the cross diminishes. Peace fades quickly when we consume ourselves with our troubles. Lord, help us to be aware of Your presence and power throughout our day, inviting You into every care that concerns us, that You may be magnified, and that we may live in Your hope and peace.

Jane Glenchur

Those who are

the happiest

are those

who do the most

for others.

Booker T. Washington

The prayer of a righteous person
is powerful and effective.

JAMES 5:16 (NIV)

Serving as chaplain coordinator at a Level 1 trauma hospital has opened my eyes to the importance of prayer. Each time I send a volunteer chaplain to visit with hospital patients, we spend time in prayer beforehand. We pray for the hospital staff, for the patients, and for the Holy Spirit to give us discernment to do and say what might bring comfort and peace to the suffering.

James 5:16 speaks about the power and effectiveness of our prayers, but James does not seem to indicate that the forcefulness with which one prays determines effectiveness. Rather, this verse points out the aspect of righteousness in the life of the supplicant. *The Message* puts it this way: *The prayer of a person living right with God is something powerful to be reckoned with.* As you seek to serve God and others, does this description fit you and your prayer life?

Rev. Rita Hays

I am like

a little pencil

in God's hand.

He does the writing.

The pencil has

nothing to do with it.

Mother Teresa

Let's not get tired of doing what is good. At just the right time we will reap a harvest of blessing if we don't give up.

GALATIANS 6:9 (NLT)

Sometimes I come home so weary that my husband insists we order take-out and suggests that I quickly go to bed! Pastoring along with chaplain ministry can easily wear and tear at the body, mind, and spirit. Once I receive some respite, I feel renewed, ready to face the challenges with revived strength.

The Christian journey is not always easy, but we have the help of the Holy Spirit who comes as our Encourager. Like the good seeds planted in the soil by a farmer confident of an abundant harvest, the seeds of our exemplary actions will eventually grow. The hard work will ultimately be worth all our efforts.

Never let anyone discourage you from doing the work of the kingdom. God created you with the ability to help others. In your weariness turn to God, who stands ready to lift you up. Always remember that you are serving Jesus Christ. By doing good, you're showing Christ to a lost and hurting world.

Rev. Rita Hays

Give what

you have.

To someone else

it may be better

than you dare

to think.

Henry Wadsworth Longfellow

Let your light shine before others, that they may… glorify your Father in heaven.

Matthew 5:16 (NIV)

The soaring walls of my childhood church were punctuated with glorious stained-glass windows. One week, our Sunday school teacher gave us a special tour of the windows. She taught us how the artist used colored glass and design to tell the stories of Jesus—not just to us, but to the world. You see, when we were sitting in the pews and the sun was shining outside, our congregation could see the images. But when the lights were turned on inside the church, everyone in our community could see the beautiful windows too! It was a way of sharing the life of Jesus with the whole neighborhood.

It's not that different with our own lives. God's light shines into our hearts, but when we let that same light shine out of us, we let the whole world see the gospel living in us. In that moment, God's glory illuminates our lives, our works, and our love, and everything points to Jesus!

Allison Lynn

I used to ask God to help me. Then I asked if I might help Him. I ended up by asking Him to do His work through me.

Hudson Taylor

I will instruct you and teach you
in the way you should go.

PSALM 32:8 (NIV)

One sunny day, I was driving down a country road when out of nowhere, I saw something shocking—cows. I live in the country, so seeing cows shouldn't be that surprising. But these particular cows were standing on the side of the road, roaming free! When they saw me in my SUV, they looked a bit surprised as well. As I made my turn onto the next country road, they followed me. When I pulled into the driveway of the farmhouse where they belonged, they ran right up to the gate of the pasture. Those cows needed some serious direction. And you know what? So do I. There are times in my life when I feel like those scared, directionless cows. Lost. Alone. And yet, instead of praying and asking the One who promises me direction, what do I do? I fret. I worry. I try to fix things myself. James 1:5 (NIV) says, *If any of you lacks wisdom, you should ask God*. The God of the Universe is willing to offer His wisdom and direction to us—all we have to do is ask!

Julie Campbell

Serve God

by doing common actions in a heavenly spirit, and then, if your daily calling only leaves you cracks and crevices of time, fill them up with holy service.

Charles Spurgeon

Peace I leave with you; my peace I give you....
Do not let your hearts be troubled.

JOHN 14:27 (NIV)

I always know my life has gotten too busy when I can no longer find my peace. Yes, adorning my nightstand, I literally have a wooden cut-out of the letters P-E-A-C-E. The only other items that are supposed to share this space are a Bible, a book light, and my reading glasses. But too often, additional things crowd the surface—my phone, a novel, sticky notes, pens, and pencils. Soon the Bible is covered up. And my P-E-A-C-E? It's gone, fallen, lying upside-down on the floor. It is no coincidence that my life at these moments often erupts with impatience, a lack of compassion, and fears about tomorrow. I must find peace. What a loving God we have. Even though we make our lives messy and neglect responding to Him, He welcomes us back. He offers us rest, contentment, and forgiveness time and again in His Word.

Miriam Lunz

I am not bound
to win,
but I am bound
to be true.
I am not bound
to succeed,
but I am bound
to live up
to what light I have.

Abraham Lincoln

The wilderness will rejoice and blossom.
Like the crocus, it will burst into bloom.

Isaiah 35:1–2 (NIV)

The garden in our new home had been ignored for years. Tall weeds choked out everything. The soil was dust. I grabbed my pruners and trowel but soon realized nothing had survived under the brambly mess. I would need to start from scratch the following spring. But as the weather warmed, little tips of green pushed through the soil. I eyed them expectantly. Almost overnight, the front yard was a carpet of crocuses! Their little stems stood at attention, topped with nodding purple heads. These delicate beauties had been smothered by strangling weeds, but with a little love and sunshine, they came back to life. We're not that different. Worries and doubts can smother us. We need to create space for the nourishment of living water and the warmth of God's loving light. What are the things we need to prune and clear away so we can grow in hope and live life to the fullest?

Allison Lynn

Faith is a living and unshakable confidence, a belief in the grace of God so assured that a man would die a thousand deaths for its sake.

Martin Luther

May the words of my mouth and the meditation of my heart be pleasing to you, O Lord.

Psalm 19:14 (NLT)

I grew up a pastor's kid. Every Sunday before my dad started to preach, he would pray the words of Psalm 19:14. It was the only time in the service that I heard my dad pray for himself, offering his thoughts and words to God. I also heard it as a prayer for each of us in the congregation, that we may somehow be open to the message we were about to hear.

It wasn't until I fell in love with the psalms that I realized this little prayer was the final verse of the lyrical Psalm 19. On first reading, this psalm has two parts. In the first half, the psalmist is praising God for the wonders of creation. In the second, the psalmist is proclaiming the beauty of God's commands.

But read it again, and you'll discover the whole psalm is about communication! Let's be aware of the words of our mouths and allow them to be pleasing to God, singing praise, and sharing love with those we serve.

Allison Lynn

No one

is useless

in this world

whose life

lightens the

burden of another.

Charles Dickens

Love the Lord your God with all your heart and with all your soul and with all your strength and with all your mind.

Luke 10:27 (NIV)

Whenever I train a new hospital chaplain as part of my work responsibilities, I remind them of the many important factors in the healing process. While chaplains provide spiritual care, we also recognize that healing involves physical and mental aspects as well. Likewise, Jesus teaches us that a healthy Christ-follower must love with the entire being: heart, body, strength, and mind. Love of God should encompass every part of our existence.

What are some practical steps we might take to put this teaching into effect? Start each day with gratitude and prayer. Begin each morning by thanking God for His love and ask the Almighty for guidance to wholeheartedly love like Jesus. It helps to keep a close watch on our thoughts, words, and actions, ensuring they reflect kindness to those we encounter daily. As we seek opportunities to serve, we discover tangible ways to show generosity to God and creation. Living out Luke 10:27 is a journey that requires dedication and constant help from the Holy Spirit.

Rev. Rita Hays

Once a saint

puts his

confidence in...God,

no tribulation

or affliction

can ever touch

that confidence.

Oswald Chambers

Tell it to your children, and let your children tell it to their children, and their children to the next generation.

Joel 1:3 (NIV)

I own my Nana's prayerbook. The cover was originally snowy white, but over the years, her hands faded it to a soft cream. The papers were edged with gold, and the shine has grown softer with each turned page. Her maiden name is stamped in the leather of the front cover, showing she received it while still a young girl, living at home with my great-grandparents. She inserted ribbons, photos, and precious keepsakes to mark her favorite passages. As I turn the silken pages, I'm immediately connected to Nana. I hear her soprano voice ringing out in the church choir. I remember her whispered prayers over me at night. I treasure the thousands of tiny ways she lived out God's love. I'm thankful for her gentle witness and for her legacy of living worship. I don't have a prayerbook to pass on, but I pray my life will be its own faith-worn testimony for the next generation.

Allison Lynn

Action springs not from thought, but from a readiness for responsibility.

Dietrich Bonhoeffer

God sent the Spirit of his Son into our hearts, the Spirit who calls out, "Abba, Father."

Galatians 4:6 (NIV)

Several years ago, my father and I hiked a mountain. We had done many hikes before, but this was the toughest one we had ever attempted. We planned to reach the summit and return to the parking lot before dark, so we took little food and only light jackets. We were on the trail at sunup and thought we would have had plenty of time, but the steep terrain slowed us down and we ran out of daylight—still miles away from the car and without flashlights. As the sun vanished over the horizon and we stood there in the dark, I called out to my father in fear: "What are we going to do? We've got to keep going!" But my father knew that there were some other hikers behind us who likely had flashlights. He encouraged me to wait, and within an hour these hikers caught up to us and we walked the rest of the way out with them. By God's Spirit in our hearts, we can cry out to God in our darkest times. Our heavenly Father will bring the light we need to move ahead.

Kevin Stiffler

The future

is purchased

at the price

of vision

in the present.

Samuel Johnson

The Lord make his face shine on you
and be gracious to you.

Numbers 6:25 (NIV)

"You have the countenance of Christ." My friend's words caught me off guard. I had never imagined possessing Christ's countenance. In fact, I had been so wrapped up in feelings of insufficiency that I didn't even think my heart resembled Christ, even if the smile on my face did. Often revisiting that memory, I have come to recognize a deep sense of peace that settles over my heart when I spend time with certain people—special friends who just seem to radiate Christ's presence. Their quietness of spirit eases the tension within my own. This truth reminds me of God's blessing on the nation of Israel in Numbers 6:24–26. God blessed the Israelites not only with His favor but also with the special hope of His peace. As believers, we have that hope in Christ. Through salvation, God can truly make His face shine upon us, filling our countenances with the radiance of hearts set free. May we lead others to this same bright hope by reflecting Christ in our lives.

Stephanie Hansen

Memories

of our lives,

of our works

and our deeds,

will continue

in others.

Rosa Parks

I do all this for the sake of the gospel,
that I may share in its blessings.

1 Corinthians 9:23 (NIV)

I love my pillow! Its spongy memory foam gives me perfect support. Give it a little spritz of lavender pillow spray, and I'm in heaven. I even take it with me when I travel! It's a bit bulky but worth the effort. With my own pillow, every bed I sleep in feels like home. But when I lay down last night, I had a thought: "Jesus never owned His own pillow." Isn't it funny the things we think about just before we go to sleep? Matthew 8:20 (NIV) tells us Jesus had no place to lay his head. As a traveling ministry, Jesus and His followers stayed in various houses, sleeping on various beds (and probably floors). They gave up all the comforts of home to bring good news to a suffering world. Looking at my pillow, I think of missionaries and ministers who, even today, give up the comforts of home for a life of ministry. I take a moment to lift them in prayer, and then ask myself, "What comfort am I willing to sacrifice to help share the gospel?"

Allison Lynn

In all ranks
of life the human
heart yearns
for the beautiful;
and the
beautiful things
that God makes
are his gift to all alike.

Harriet Beecher Stowe

Here I am! I stand at the door and knock.

REVELATION 3:20 (NIV)

When I was a teenager, I was a student leader for both my church youth group and the Campus Life group at my high school. I really enjoyed these roles, but I often found myself volunteering and striving to the point of burn out. I ended up feeling tired and unfulfilled in my relationship with Christ. When I talked about what I was feeling with my youth leader, he said to me, "Being busy isn't going to bring you closer to God. Slow down and open your heart to Him."

My gut instinct is to make everything into a goal, something to be accomplished, and then work hard to accomplish it. And while it's important to serve and to use our gifts to further God's kingdom and spread the gospel, those things aren't going to bring us any closer to God. He's already close. He's waiting on us to open our hearts to Him. We don't have to seek and strive; all we have to do is open the door.

Liz Flinn

You have not lived today until you have done something for someone who can never repay you.

John Bunyan

Don't worry about anything;
instead, pray about everything.

PHILIPPIANS 4:6 (NLT)

Susanna Wesley was the mother of John and Charles Wesley, founders of the Methodist movement and hugely influential in the spiritual life of England. Susanna had 19 children—yes, you read that right, *nineteen* (sadly, 9 of her children died in infancy). If anyone had an excuse to be too busy to pray, it was Susanna Wesley. But instead of making excuses, she devoted herself to two hours of prayer a day!

As you can imagine, she struggled to find a quiet place to pray. So she came up with her own unique "prayer closet." When she wanted to spend time in prayer, Susanna would sit down in her kitchen and throw her apron over her head. Her children knew not to disturb her when she was praying. No doubt, her prayers were part of the reason her sons were able to bring millions of souls to Christ. Susanna's devotion to God continues to be an inspiration to me. Our prayers for others really can make a difference and change the world!

Julie Campbell

It's not how much we give, but how much love we put into giving.

Mother Teresa

My God shall supply all your need according to his riches in glory by Christ Jesus.

Philippians 4:19 (KJV)

The little red arrow was inching nearer to that dreaded E. I knew we should have filled up after lunch. As the tank got closer to empty, my anxiety got closer to overflow. Suddenly, a tall sign reached above the trees. A gas station was one exit away! I prayed the drops in the bottom of our tank would be enough. Just as the red arrow finally touched the E, I pulled up to the tank and turned off the car. We'd made it. How many times are we like this in our spiritual lives? We plow through life, thinking we can make it on our own. We ignore the warning signs that our fuel is getting low and then wonder why we're struggling. But unlike our close call on the highway, we don't need to hunt for a gas station. Our Source is always close at hand, ready to fill us with strength, hope, and peace. God's supply is unlimited and always exactly what we need.

Allison Lynn

Where you go
or what you do
is not nearly
as important
as Whom you serve.

Rebecca Barlow Jordan

All glory to God, who is able…to accomplish infinitely more than we might ask or think.

Ephesians 3:20 (NLT)

On February 8, 2023, following a regularly scheduled chapel service at Asbury University, revival broke out. It all started when a fellow student decided to confess his sins to some classmates. Worship continued and prayer resumed. Soon others heard about the gathering and joined in praise. The revival lasted for more than two weeks, drawing about 15,000 worshipers a day.

God moves in mysterious ways. Luke 1:37 (KJV) reads, *With God nothing shall be impossible*. Do you believe those words? Or do you sometimes think there are things not possible for God to accomplish in our world, our churches, and our lives? Believing in the promise of these words does not mean that God will always grant all our wishes. Rather, it affirms that we see a God unlimited to our way of thinking and acting.

Ponder the many ways you have experienced God working in impossible situations of life. Be on the lookout for God's surprising work and extraordinary ministry in your life and the lives of others. And give glory to God!

Rev. Rita Hays

Life's most persistent and urgent question is, What are you doing for others?

Dr. Martin Luther King Jr.